THREE STEPS

TO

INSPIRATION

FOR LIFE

THREE STEPS

TO

INSPIRATION

FOR LIFE

BY BASS TADROS

CONSCIOUS CARE PUBLISHING PTY LTD

THREE STEPS TO INSPIRATION FOR LIFE

Copyright © 2017 by Bass Tadros. All rights reserved.

First Published 2017 by: Conscious Care Publishing Pty Ltd
33 Crompton Road, Rockingham, WA 6168, Australia
PO Box 776, Rockingham, WA 6968, Australia
Phone: (61+) 1300 814 115   www.consciouscarepublishing.com

Second Edition printed April 2017.

Notice of Rights

This book is sold subject to the condition that it shall not, by way of trade or otherwise, be lent, resold, hired out, or otherwise circulated without the publisher's prior consent, in any form of binding or cover, other than that in which it is published, and without a similar condition, including this condition being imposed on the subsequent purchaser. All rights reserved by the publisher. No part of this publication may be reproduced, stored in a retrieval system, or transmitted in any form, or by any means, electronic, digital, mechanical, photocopying, scanning, recorded or otherwise, without the prior written permission of the copyright owner. Requests to the copyright owner should be addressed to Permissions Department, Conscious Care Publishing Pty Ltd, PO Box 776, Rockingham, WA 6968, Australia, Phone: (61+) 1300 814 115 or email admin@consciouscarepublishing.com

Categories
1. Self Help. 2. New Age. 3. Mind, Body, Spirit   4. Relationships.

Limits of Liability/Disclaimer of Warranty:

While the publisher and author have used their best efforts in preparing this book, they make no representations or warranties with respect to the accuracy or completeness of the contents of this book and specifically disclaim any implied warranties of merchantability or fitness for a particular purpose. No warranty may be created or extended by sales representatives or written sales materials. The author of this book does not dispense medical advice or prescribe the use of any technique as a form of treatment for physical, emotional, or medical problems without the advice of a physician, either directly or indirectly. The advice and strategies contained herein may not be suitable for your situation. You should consult with a professional where appropriate. The intent of the author is only to offer information for a general nature to help you in your request for a happier life. Neither the publisher nor author shall be liable for any loss of profit or any other commercial damages, including but not limited to special, incidental, consequential, or other damages. The author and the publisher assume no responsibility for your actions.

Conscious Care Publishing publishes in a variety of print and electronic format and by print-on-demand. Some material included with standard print versions of this book may not be included in e-books or in print-on-demand. If this book refers to media such as a CD or DVD that is not included in the version you purchased, you may download this material at www.consciouscarepublishing.com.

National Library of Australia Cataloguing-in-Publication entry:
Author: Tadros, Bass, 1981-
Three Steps to Inspiration for Life / by Bass Tadross
ISBN 9780994540430 (Paperback), 9780648085409 (eBook)
Tadros, Bass, 1981-
Liz Atherton, Editor

Printed by Lightning Source
Typeset & cover design by Conscious Care Publishing Pty Ltd

158.1

ISBN: 978-0-9945404-3-0

To you,
my reader, for
embracing your
true potential

DR. JOHN DEMARTINI SAYS...

"*Three Steps to Inspiration for Life* by Bass Tadros offers you a simple, easy to follow, three step, strategic personal and professional guide on how to be inspired while doing what you love and loving what you do and while making a difference through awakening your creative inner genius."

Dr John Demartini – International bestselling author of *The Values Factor*.

We all want to be inspired. But what is inspiration exactly?

Bass Tadros

CONTENTS

Preface	1
Acnowlegements	5
Introduction	7
Step One: Internal Wisdom	11
Step Two: Power of Mindfulness	37
Step Three: Know Thyself - Connection	49
Closing Reflections	57
About the Author	61
Selected Bibliography	65

PREFACE

WHAT TO EXPECT FROM THREE STEPS TO INSPIRATION FOR LIFE

We are all capable of greatness, the path ahead of us is clear and the way is lit. All we need to do is decide to proceed and take the first step, a leap of faith the rest is a natural flow after that first step
- Bass Tadross

Prepare yourself for some views and ideals that will help you reflect and guide you on a path that you might already be familiar with, if you're not familiar with the entire path you will be familiar with at the very least certain parts of it. The first point, which is vital to getting us in the right mindset is to understand and be in complete belief that we are born with an innate ability that contains all the resources we will need on our life's journey and with the wisdom we require for growth and living a great life to the absolute most.

Have you ever found yourself searching and yearning for more, more knowledge more money, perhaps a pay rise, and more connection more love?

That's all part of the knowing from within that is constantly telling you that you deserve more and that you are capable of more. There are a few reasons that lead to a disconnect with that innate wisdom, the reasons vary, but are relative to each person and situation. We will explore what propels us towards inspiration and what holds us back from being inspiring to others and ourselves. It could be that people reach a point where they feel comfortable so they stagnate, or they keep getting knocked back from a promotion, or they feel stuck or hurt from something or someone, perhaps a sad ending to a relationship, feeling of loss or grief.

People hold themselves back by comparing themselves to others or having limiting beliefs that they are not even aware of that are holding them back from making progress.

That said; we all need to understand that although we may not be perfect, we are all doing the best we can with what we have right now and what we know or think we know to be true for us at this point in our life.

Ideas in this book will be challenging yet inspirational. With the purpose of drawing on the principles used for designing and activating our true potential. Insights on our inner wisdom, the mind's processing power and the phenomenal power of our thoughts.

FREE GIFT!

I love giving and offering value to everyone I have any interactions with. Be it online or face to face here is a gift for acquiring my book. Enjoy the book and I look forward to connecting with you. This gift certificate is my way of serving as many people as I can. My grand vision is to impact as many as 200,000,000 lives. Yes, that's 200 million people. All you have to do is tear out the certificate at the rear of the book and book an appointment.

ACKNOWLEGEMENTS

Thank you to all the people that have been an inspiration to me. I have been fortunate to write this book, whilst travelling around Australia, South East Asia and India.

A big thank you to my mentors and source of great inspiration for your insightful guidance in both my life.

All my friends, clients and students that have given me the opportunity to share my joy and life purpose with the world.

My beautiful wife and precious son, who have taught me what it means to be a husband and father.

My three sisters, who taught me to honour sisterhood.

Last but not least, to my loving and hard working parents, for always believing in me and for being always ready and willing to make sacrifies, giving up so much to allow me to have the opportunities I have today. All the love you shared also gave me reasons to pursue my cause and living a life of purpose and passion. You will forever be my greatest teachers.. May we forever be connected through love.

And to those I am yet to meet, may your paths lead you to the place of greatest peace and abundant inspiration.

INTRODUCTION

When we search for inspiration all roads lead to one place, that place is within each and every one of us. You already knew that, just as you already know that picking up a book cannot change your life or can it? It may change your views or ideas about life through a new perspective if you are open to change. Change needs to come from within as no one can change who we are, only we can make a change in ourselves.

Just like change inspiration needs to be recognised as something we have absolute control over as it comes from within.

Put simply inspiration is a feeling that you must be open to so that you may feel truly inspired.

I am drawing on experiences that provided my knowledge and wisdom far beyond the limits of initial perceptions – this, we all share and it connects us.

This knowledge is first hand and is not imposed by other teachings and or beliefs so I invite you to question ideas presented and look at this with your own system of being a wonderful truly analytical being, as that will help you take in important lessons beyond surface value.

Dig deep and in order to gain the gains, be open – open up your heart and mind to the three steps of uncovering your inspiration for life through insight, mindfulness and connection.

Introduction

This book reveals my personal inspirations that have enabled me to overcome the setbacks of being a perfectionist, set in my own ways and overcoming my fear of failure.

Sharing these thoughts with you will provide you with guidance as well as inspiration to live according to your highest values.

STEP ONE:

INTERNAL WISDOM - INSIGHT

Inspiration comes from within, what I am referring to is the wise voice from within each and every one of us. You know that voice - the one that you seek when you're in need of guidance. It's a positive voice, a voice that is reassuring and kind. Some call it "Intuition" and some call it "The Third Eye".

It was first introduced to me as "The Holy Spirit"

by my mother as a child.

We all have it. It's a matter of trusting that voice. Once you listen to the voice it becomes more noticeable to and it will guide you towards growth.

> *But the fruit of the Spirit is love, joy, peace, forbearance, kindness, goodness, faithfulness, gentle-ness and self-control. Against such things there is no law.*
> - **Galatians 5:22-23**

Throughout life, through many lifetimes, many generations, those who have been inspirationally successful at whatever it is they have set their mind to, predominantly trusted in the guidance that they had from within.

They followed that instinct, chased that dream, acted on that thought and reached their success.

On the other hand, those who are caught up

in doubt and or fear have neglected to pay attention to that voice. The more they neglected the voice the less the voice became predominant in their life. You see it's like anything. The more you nurture a plant, a person, a relationship, a business, even a thought or an idea the more it grows.

Have you had inspirational ideas of late that grew into a plan?

Did you act on them?

If you find yourself fascinated by a new idea, chances are there's something meaningful about it for you to consider.

Fascination is nature's way of getting our attention and getting us fired up leading to inspiration.

Well beyond infatuation, it's an indication that we are being called. Out of the thousands of ideas with the power to capture our imagination, the felt fascination for one of the ideas is a clue that there's something worthy of our engagement.

Don't dismiss it as trivial. Give it room.

Give it time to breathe. Honour it and it will grow possibly leading to amazing inspiration.

Follow your curiosity down the path into the subject or thing that most fascinates you. Your deepest interests and even obsessions provide a clue that something significant is knocking on the door of your unconscious mind. When we have the will to allow fascination to grow inside us the illogical suddenly becomes logical and the miraculous is pregnant with possibilities.

Here is one of my fascinations. One morning I woke up thinking we all want to be inspired. But what is inspiration exactly?

What does inspiration mean? I found myself digging deep and wanting to share my findings in order to inspire others.

Inspiration means literally, "to breathe in and be filled with spirit".

According to the ancient Greeks who believed inspiration to mean; to breathe in and be filled with spirit with the spirit of the gods.

The gods were the muses of ancient

Greece. Greek myth explained that all creativity came from the gods and that mortals (that's us) can only receive somewhat imperfect copies of the originals.

I believe our creator made us in his image therefore we can in our own way be creative and inspiring, the only limit is what we put on ourselves.

The modern meaning of inspiration is a motivating action or influence that results in creative works and productivity of all kinds. We all depend on inspiration and in an acknowledgement of the Greek origins of inspiration, they sometimes refer to someone who inspires them as a Muse. We gaze on our creations with amusement.

Whenever I start something new, I know I have a lot to learn – in fact this encourages me and gives me energy.

Energy that keeps me "child-like" – how, by being open... being adventurous. Being curious. Being eager to learn.

Free of judgments or preconceived ideas. Acknowledge the wonder of life and the amazing experience it brings through learning.

I recall a quote I love by bestselling author and leadership expert John Maxwell.

"Change is inevitable, growth is optional."

We all know that the only constant in life is change and if you want to get a different result from your life to what your currently getting you have to change your thinking – begin to think differently, to create different beliefs.

We will address beliefs, but first we need to look at the "will". We all have the power of free will, are we willing to take our first step in creating our inspirational future?

I know you are excited about transforming your life. I know you want it more than anything...

But are you willing - I mean REALLY willing - to be different? Be more inspirational?

Here's the truth – to have a different life, you have to be totally different than you have ever been before. You have to be the person that has the life you want, and I can pretty much guarantee that is going to seriously push your comfort zone.

Let's start by taking small steps. Can you recall a time when you were really inspired can you recall what you saw, what you heard yourself or others say that made you believe that you were inspired or you inspiring to someone.

Thinking of when you were last inspired, can be a good place to start to get inspired again just by thinking of that experience as you recall it and your memory goes there you begin to feel a sense of what inspiration feels like to you.

Over the next few pages, we will not just be covering what thoughts lead to inspiration, but we will cover why it is that some people are inspired and others have a self-destructive pattern that seems to be on auto repeat and they wonder why they are not achieving the results they want in life.

I am a big believer that in order to be really inspired and inspirational one must absolutely be congruent.

What does "Congruent" really mean?

Two of the many inspirational people I look up to are Sir Richard Branson and Robert

Kiyosaki. What they both have in common in my observation of their success and leadership styles, is that they are both congruent. When I work with conscious leaders I often observe how present and aligned they are in what they are doing at any point in time, people have said the following about congruent leaders that they been observed thinking, speaking then taking those actions in most instances where all three are aligned.

Many of us know people who are incongruent. They think one thing, say something else, and do not do what they say or think. I have observed these kind of conflicted people, achieve limited success and live unobtainable goals.

This really integrates into my life transformation, because I can relate to times in my life where I was congruent in my thinking, words and actions reflected exactly what I had set out to achieve.

On the other hand I had several experiences where I struggled to get simple plans off the ground and that was at a time where I felt that I had at least two parts of me that screamed opposing ideas, "YES" do it and the other was silently pulling me in the opposite direction. The only way to come to terms with this is to work out what the purpose is behind each of those two parts of our thinking, at a deeper level we need to ask ourselves 'why we are having opposing thoughts, why they are opposing each other and what the greatest good is behind each of them?' and bring them to harmony in order to be congruent.

At times this can lead to procrastination or indecision. Great leaders and most inspirational people are not afraid to make a decision, one way or another making a decision at the very least leads to an outcome. Once you have an outcome you can then learn from it whether it was a good decision or otherwise. We will get into specifics, as we delve deeper as you learn how. To be more congruent you can apply it to any area in your life to see inspirational results. Let's cover fear and doubts, which are elements of effect that limit inspiration, we can get the roadblocks out of the way.

Did you know that the only two fears we are born with are the fear of falling and loud noises? Two fears. Every other fear is learnt at some point in our early stages of development and can be unlearned if we put our mind to it. So all other fears that we have decided to take on may have been there for a reason to serve us at some stage. However just as we have made the decision at a point in our life where we needed to have that particular feeling we can at any point decide to remove that fear.

Yes that's right it's just a decision. So all we need to do is decide on when would be the best time to acknowledge that although a certain fear has served us in a way, now is the time where we can remove that road block, as it may no longer serve us if it's a limiting belief.

When I was a child of about nine years of age I feared jumping in the deep end of the pool, I had no idea why at the time, but I attributed myself to not being a confident swimmer. This was a huge setback for me at that age because I enjoyed being in the water and this fear meant I could not do what my friends where doing with diving in the deep end and going on the slippery slides.

As I got to my teens I broke through that fear because a friend assured me that I can jump in the deep end and be safe so long as I paddle and hold onto the edge to the edge of the pool I would be fine. Once I gave it a shot there was no stopping me, I really enjoyed getting through that debilitating fear, because after all I really loved the water. Once I got through it, I thought what was all that fear and panic about? I tried to recall if I had a previous bad experience and drew a blank.

One day in a more reflective state of mind I remembered what caused me to have that fear was an experience at the beach when I was about five or so years of age possibly younger, I watched my younger sister nearly drown and that memory was more of my mother's reaction and her fear of the event,. My sister certainly established a fear of swimming in deeper water from that experience too, her experience must have been far more dramatic than mine after all she lived that frightening event I just got a glimpse of it from a distance as I was in shallow waters, so my fear at that time was learnt from watching her and mum react to the situation.

Fears can be regarded as a protection that we sometimes put in place in order to remove us out of a certain situation or confrontation that we don't want to be faced with. Just as we've decided to place that fear, we can at any stage in our lives decide to remove it naturally. Though we seem to have a set and forget kind of system, if we are intuitive enough and listen to that internal voice, we would sometimes pick up on what it is that we need to remove and at what point exactly it needs to be removed.

That's not to say, that without intuitiveness we wouldn't pick up on it at all, but it's to say that we'd pick up on it earlier, before it sets us back or prevents us from missing opportunities that we would otherwise be open to.

Pause and reflect: what opportunities have you knowingly missed due to a fear? You might have a fear of heights so you've turned down a parachute diving experience with a friend.

So assuming that you are aware of your fear

of heights you'd be aware that you've turned it down for that reason, but what if you were not aware that you have a fear of heights but continuously turned down fun adventures or even job opportunities that might require exposure to heights.

Can you see how fear limits your options or even considerations of certain things, if I had a fear of height I might not even consider a job that involved flying, be it as an airplane pilot etc.

While we are on the topic of fear, we can observe that fear really can be debilitating. It can be regarded as the opposite to inspiration, because it is a prevention of living life to the most of what we were intended to do. You see when you're inspired you're unstoppable, you proceed with purpose to achieve the outcome and results that you have in mind. On the other hand, fear can be lurking in the background of your unconscious mind preventing you from taking any course of action at all to pursue an outcome or result you really want to achieve.

All you have to do is focus on what you want. I can't take away your fears and doubts no matter how many pages I write. You will just need to trust yourself and the power within you that you can truly follow your inspiration and do things in a way that brings you joy and have it all work out the way you imagine it to play out in your mind.

Take Action!

One morning, I was invited to a workshop. It was a workshop about NLP. When I arrived, there was a setup of books and audio CDs displayed for purchase. My first thought was to purchase one of the books however without even realising I talked myself out of it and took a seat. As the workshop started, the presenter who's a very intuitive and inspirational man started talking about taking action.

He proceeded with a simple and clear instruction – that if we (the audience) are to learn about taking action we need to take action now.

His instructions were for the first three people to get up and take action by grabbing one of his books, he also stated that he would have an incentive for them.

I heard myself say in my mind "what have I got to lose?" I wanted to get one of these books to begin with, so what's holding me back?" Just as I finished that thought, I realised that I had already got up and acted – I had one of his books in my hand. Before I returned back to my seat, he approached me and said "congratulations you were the first to take action. That book is your reward".

As I sat down I was grateful for the book yet more grateful for the lesson. As I reflected in the moment, there was a priceless; the lesson was that I need to take action and stop allowing my limiting beliefs from talking me out of things I need to do, to gain life inspiring experience. I wondered what else I haven't been acting on in my life and what had prevented me from taking action.

Upon further reflection I realised that I talked myself out of buying the book when I first entered the room, because I had an image I played in my mind of all the books on my bookshelf that I hadn't picked up in ages.

As a result of that image my thoughts were 'what's the point in buying this book if I never have time to read? So as I reflected I had one of those moments, where I questioned "why?"

Why don't I make time to read? Then I thought while I'm at it, now that

I have this lesson fresh in my mind and my reward this new book is in my hand, I am going to make a plan. I am going to plan to make time and start reading my new book and get past my old limitation due to a self-imposed belief, coincidentally the new book happened to have the title "Life beyond Limits" by Rik Schnabel.

> *"At times our own light goes out and is rekindled by a spark from another person. Each of us has cause to think with deep gratitude of those who have lit the flame within"*

Coincident or fate – life has ways of throwing us some guidance, but after all if I didn't take action I would not know any different.

Sure enough my plan to make time to read came to fruition and in the first sitting I read about five chapters into this book, which inspired me to read on. I was so exhilarated that I had done so much reading for as long as I could remember I wanted to make time to read, but now I was actually doing it and enjoying thanks to planning and taking action. I made another plan to read all of it by a set time frame.

This is the only book I had ever read from cover to cover at that point so I sensed a feeling of accomplishment. Sure I had read lots of short e-books and manuals, but the inspiration to read a book from cover to cover was not only perceived to be daunting for me but also I had made so many excuses to back my limiting thoughts up so I don't take action to read; excuses where wide and varied ranging from - am such an active person that making time to sit and read is not possible, now I know that it used to be challenging but not impossible to sit still and read for a while after all I love learning.

ADJUST YOUR BELIEFS

Believe you are smarter, and you'll become smarter. For this, affirmations may work, but even better is evidence.

Make a note of your successes. Tell yourself, "Hey, that was really creative," when you do something creative. When you have a good idea, make a note of it. Gather the evidence for your own intelligence and you'll start to experience more of it.

OVERCOMING OUR SELF-IMPOSED BARRIERS

We sometimes sabotage ourselves without knowing - through things like stubbornness, procrastination and false limiting beliefs; one of my false limiting beliefs as mentioned earlier was that I had no time to read, that reading is not for me, I am too active to sit down and read a book. All I had to do was notice that I was talking myself out of doing something I required to continue my growth and then I took action and made a plan.

The power of planning is incredible to ensure

you achieve desired outcomes to make things happen and when I did, it changed my way of thinking I gained massive learning and growth. In Step two we'll see how we can overcome self-imposed barriers for good through the power of mindfulness, but first we need to take a quick look at the importance of FOCUS.

Do you "Focus" on what you don't have?

Have you ever agonised over a shortage of anything, most people tend to worry about money? Have you worried obsessively about not being able to pay your bills or buy something you wanted?

How inspired did this make you feel?

Believe it or not, you were probably making the situation worse by doing so. We know that lack is the condition of not having something you want – in other words, the absence of something. Lack is not the absence of money, or health, or love.

Those are just the symptoms of lack. At its core, lack is simply the blockage of ENERGY. When it comes right down to it, everything is energy.

When you experience lack of any kind, it's a sure sign that you are cutting off the natural flow of energy through your life.

Every time you worry about your financial situation, agonise over a shortage of money, or feel stressed about your bills, you attract more of the experience of lack into your life.

Gratitude is more powerful as you Focus on What You DO Have and attract what you DO Want.

It may sound incredibly difficult to focus on the positive when your life doesn't look so rosy, but it is vital to find a way to do it. When you focus on the good things you already have and think about the things you want from an optimistic and hopeful state of mind, you cannot help but attract more of them into your life.

There are endless ways to begin focusing your thoughts on the things you do have and do want. Start a gratitude list of a few things each day that you are grateful for. The more you focus on things you're grateful for the more they will begin to show up in your actual reality.

Step One: Internal Wisdom - Insight

STEP TWO:

POWER OF MINDFULNESS

Taking Ownership of your Conscious William James philosopher and psychologist - Observed the greatest discovery that; by changing the inner aspects of our thinking we can change the outer aspects of our lives. Upon this statement is the truth that we are not victims of our situation but the creators of our reality and of the world around us. So we can choose to think we are victims to our life and situation, effected by all that goes on.

Or choose to think we are in control and we have an impact on our lives through the power of our thoughts, which lead to empowering actions and living for the cause.

People that live in the cause are powerful people who take responsibility for their lives and don't hand over the power through blame. The moment we blame someone else we hand over our power and lose control of that situation. I chose to think that every moment I felt angry or upset I actually could have prevented or at least controlled it from escalating and that it was no one else's fault but mine. I allowed myself to get worked up.

No one can make us feel anything we don't want to feel, yet we sometimes chose to get all worked up and say "so and so" made my angry. Of course people test us, or they can be difficult at times to the point where we start seeing red and think the only realistic response to this is to get mad and angry. That's in the heat of the moment, but is an angry reaction really the best solution? Is it a well thought out response? I think it's a reaction we tend to refer to, as it's a quick self-protecting mechanism, a thoughtless reaction.

The sooner we learn to be mindful, control our thinking the sooner we become resourceful and we can tap in to being not only inspiring, but peaceful and loving.

WHY MINDFULLNESS?

Mindfulness means focusing your awareness on the present moment more than on your inner dialogue.

Being mindful lets you move beyond the energy wasting tendencies of distress over past events or worry about future possibilities, and into the only place where you have any mental power – your now.

The greatest obstacle to inspiration or happiness for that matter is not living in the present moment and not following your joy. The solution is to do just the opposite. If you find yourself focusing on the past or the future, remind yourself that the present moment is all there is, and then surrender to what is and see how life suddenly starts working for you.

If you put the same amount of effort into finding what gives you joy as you put into going to work at a job you dislike, you will end up with results that will make you think, "why did I wait so long to do this?"

With a regular practice of mindfulness, you'll begin to observe and understand your internal experiences. When you stop and notice these experiences, you can learn from them, leading to a greater capacity to manage your mind and emotions more effectively.

Amazing how our minds work, we are always searching for answers right wrong or indifferent we are always searching for meaning.. "Why?" I find myself compelled to ask that, because we are meaning making machines – it is said that as Homo sapiens we are meaning seeking beings the main questions that every reflective individual asks are; who am I? Why am I here? How shall I live?

I am not going to delve deep to attempt to answer these questions however; I can simply state that this is one of the reasons why religion continues to play a great role in our society, as it has always been the greatest source of meaning from the beginning of time.

Although the concept of mindfulness through meditation has roots from Buddhism, it's actually very similar to practices found in other religions, particularly Christianity. But I want to point out that, despite these historical connections to religion, mindfulness is generally taught today with no religious overlay, and pursued by people of all faiths because of the benefits it offers.

Now knowing that we are searching for meaning, "seek and you shall find" in other words ask a question and your mind will go on a hunt for the answers.

This is important to understand about ourselves as human beings. Why you ask? Well the moment I learned if I ask a question even in my deepest thoughts, my mind would go searching for the answers. I started to monitor what questions and thoughts I allow myself to contemplate. Because if the questions are not well thought through, the mind will find answers. Even though, sometimes even though the answers are not real, true or accurate we own them and because they are our own thoughts we created them as we in our mind came up with them we want to believe them and why you ask??

Because we like to be right, I came up with the answer and I am sticking to it.

Have you found yourself ever thinking that way?

Here's how it works: your thoughts trigger your emotions. Your emotional state emits a specific energy to the universe, and life returns events and experiences into your day to day existence, that correspond with your emotional frequency.

When you think and feel positively on a regular basis, everything in your life seems to flow more easily, including money. When your thoughts and emotions lean more toward the negative side on a regular basis, you experience more problems, setbacks and financial lack in your life. Also important are your beliefs as mentioned earlier. Your beliefs form the structure of what is possible for you. If you believe you have to work hard to have a lot of money, you'll create exactly that experience for yourself.

If you don't believe you deserve more than a certain amount of money, you'll block more from arriving. Whatever your beliefs are, they are your TRUTH, and you will subconsciously create evidence that supports that truth over and over again until you learn to do things differently.

If I get out of bed and I ask myself in the morning 'why do I feel so great and energetic?', my mind will go into autopilot and within microseconds it will give me a few answers that go something like this.

Well I got a good restful sleep or I had an awesome dream. Now if I asked the question differently I would have an entirely different answer. Let's say the question was 'why do, I feel so unhappy or un-rested?', the answers would be flowing again automatically, but this time they will be backing up the fact that I am unhappy and unrested. The point here is to state questions and thoughts in the positive and our amazing mind will find ways and reasons to back that positively leading to greater more elevated feelings or emotions. The opposite is true, go ahead try it now if you like. Ask yourself why you don't look good today.

The answers will start coming up as: I am having a bad hair day, I rushed when I applied my makeup, or I haven't shaved, I need a haircut, I have bags under my eyes because I haven't had much sleep etc. The mind goes on a spin searching for reasons to back up your ideas. How would that leave you feeling, well you wouldn't rush up and start meeting new people or get all excited and inspired. Now if that was simply phrased a little different as you asked why do I look good or feel good?

The answers would be because; my eyes stand out in this colour top, it could be the new hair style, and the list goes on. Now you could be smiling as you start to find your emotions feel elevated and you starting not only looking good but feeling good about yourself and your appearance. Thanks to the power of asking and thinking in a mindful kind-of way, our thinking then goes to find the answers / reasons to back that trail of thinking leaving us feeling really good with heightened emotions. The ability to physiologically change, or 're-tune' your brain for enhanced compassion may be mindfulness' greatest gift to humanity, but it certainly isn't the only one. Mindfulness is a way of attuning your mind to develop a different (and less reactive, less distressing) relationship with your thoughts, feelings, and sensations.

By changing the inner aspects of our

thinking we can change the outer aspects of our lives.
– William James philosopher and psychologist

When you begin to bring self-awareness into your life through a regular practice of mindfulness, it changes you from the inside out. This is a means of 'taking ownership' of your thoughts, feelings and actions. The results are priceless. Adding simple mindfulness exercises to your day can make the difference between living your life in a state of stress or fear, to living in control of your emotions.

MINDFULNESS EXERCISES

Concentration and clear thinking are more or less automatic once you remove distractions. Learn to stop and watch your busy mind. As you notice things that are subtly bothering you, deal with them. This might mean making a phone call you need to make, or putting things on a list so you can forget them for now. With practice, this becomes easier, and you're thinking becomes more powerful.

STEP THREE:

KNOW THYSELF - CONNECTION

Being an inspirational being We are all capable of being inspired and inspiring others I have always known the importance of having the ability to be a team player, growing up as the eldest child within my family unit as well as participating at school in team sports like soccer and football I learnt the value each member of a team or a family can have on making an overall impact on the results or outcomes.

Even in the corporate world and as an entrepreneur I see this every day.

In a big sense, we're all in this together, and thinking otherwise won't give us the results we might be aiming for. More than ever, working together is integral to survival as well as to success.

> *When you have once seen the glow of happiness on the face of a beloved person, you know that a man can have no vocation but to awaken that light on the faces surrounding him. In he depth of winter, I finally learned that within me there lay an invincible summer.*

SELF-AWARENESS

Step Three: Know Thyself - Connection

This may not seem as important to us as brainpower, but it is a vital piece of the puzzle. When we know ourselves better, we can avoid the usual effects of ego and emotion in our seemingly "rational" thinking. Or we can at least take it into account.

Watch ourselves especially as we explain things or argue a point. We have all heard it said; we need to first learn to love ourselves before we can to learn to love others. The same can be said about inspiration, acceptance, understanding and connection. We connect better with others once we are well connected within ourselves through better self-awareness.

I can now say with confidence, the only things that will satisfy the soul are gratitude and love. What else is there without that? If we want to evolve spiritually, we don't need to get rid of the ego or even overcome the ego. We simply need to learn how to access the part of ourselves that is already beyond the ego.

My observation of being beyond my ego came from early childhood, from a young age my parents taught me to love and express gratitude as frequently and as regularly as possible. That love helps with being humble, kind and giving.

Emmet Fox put it so well when he said,

"Sufficient realization of love will overcome anything. There is no difficulty that love cannot conquer, no disease it will not heal, no door it will not open, no guilt it will not bridge, no wall it will not tear down, no sin it will not redeem.

Love will lift you to the highest dimension."

I love everything I do. I love my work. I love giving, sharing teaching. And I love writing this book for you!

We all need to learn to love and accept ourselves, as we are capable of being more. We can only be compassionate and understanding of others to the degree we are compassionate and understanding of ourselves. So instead of judging we can be accepting and kind to others and ourselves.

We see in others qualities that we possess or have possessed.

Once we love others as they are, others will have the opportunity to be reciprocal in their own way.

Connection through humility.

Once we are humble we open up to accepting others and ourselves for whom we are and this acceptance leads to deeper connection.

We all have our own view our own opinion whether our views align or not it's not important, what is important is that we respect the views of others enough to not dismiss their importance if it doesn't line up with our own.

THREE STEPS TO INSPIRATION FOR LIFE

We cannot live only for ourselves. A thousand fibres connect us with our fellow men; and among those fibres, as sympathetic threads, our actions run as causes, and they come back to us as effects.
- Herman Melville

Coming together is a beginning, keeping together is progress, working together is success.
- Henry Ford

When you have once seen the glow of happiness on the face of a beloved person, you know that a man can have no vocation but to awaken that light on the faces surrounding him. In the depth of winter, I finally learned that within me there lay an invincible summer.
- Albert Camus

Step Three: Know Thyself - Connection

*Humankind has not woven the web of life.
We are but one thread within it. Whatever
we do to the web, we do to ourselves.
All things are bound together. All things
connect.*
- Chief Seattle

*It really boils down to this: that all life
is interrelated. We are all caught in an
inescapable network of mutuality, tired
into a single garment of destiny. Whatever
affects one destiny, affects all indirectly.*
- Martin Luther King Jr.

CLOSING REFLECTIONS

The greatest news of all is that you don't have to do a thing to find inspiration or peace on this wild magical world apart from tune into and connect with your inner being. You can naturally relax into who you are right now. This roller coaster we call life will still take you up and down, being relaxed, you will remain calm, focused, grounded and centred which will lead you to inspiration effortlessly.

When you are centred you naturally release any unsatisfying repetitive negative thoughts and behaviours.

To find inspiration, simply stop striving to get somewhere better than here, what you haven't got you don't really need right now or perhaps it is not missing at all you have it in some other form and you just need to be open to seeing it from a new perspective. Stop trying to become someone super special. As you already are that and more. By tuning in you will see, hear and feel just how amazing of a being you really are. You can just relax into this experience and let your wisdom guide you.

When you relax into yourself, the abundance of love that you are naturally flows out into the world.

I invite you to spend a few minutes today to

meditate on welcoming the roller coaster ride of life.

ABOUT THE AUTHOR

BASS TADROS - THOUGHT LEADER & CONFIDENCE THERAPIST

Bass Tadros has worked for the past 12 years with multinational organisations specialising in Marketing, Communication and Planning. Bass has led teams of professionals in Australia and internationally through successful and seamless change work. Bass is the author of "Three Steps To Inspiration For Life" and the founder of For Life Coaching & Hypnotherapy. He is dedicated to helping people identify and shift the unseen forces that are holding them back from achieving desired results in business and personally. He does this by drawing on over a decade of experience in communication, planning and aligning people to processes that get tangible results.

Beyond coaching, the preferred approach is to silence the mind and utilise hypnotic, heart centring technics that get fast effective lasting impact for clients, both in business and personal matters.

Why is Hypnotherapy effective?

Hypnotherapy utilises the hypnotic and psychotherapeutic techniques to explore and resolve issues. When a client is hypnotised, the appropriate and relevant suggestions are given or a number of metaphors that directly communicate with the un-conscious mind. This

About the Author

process allows you to achieve your goals and bring about the changes you are looking for. It is widely recognised that suggestions made in hypnotherapy help to establish new ways of thinking and behaving. Hypnotherapy creates new patterns that reduce and replace negative thoughts, habits and unhelpful internal chatter, resolving inner conflicts and leaving you free to move on.

Bass is dedicated to creating a legacy of transformational inspiring impact with his extensive and diverse client base.

For more information on Bass and his upcoming free mindset workshops please visit www.basstadros.com or on Facebook at https://www.facebook.com/BassTadros/

Please join the movement "Love Again" on facebook at: https://www.facebook.com/groups/LoveAgainMovement/

Together we can support people that need to love again, their body, their partner, their life.

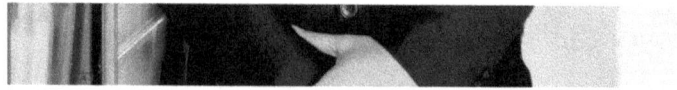

SELECTED BIBLIOGRAPHY

Schnabel, Rik. Life beyond Limits. Brolga Publishing 2006.

Blair, Lawrence. Rhythms of Vision: The Changing Patterns of Belief. Schocken Books 1976.

Carroll, Lenedra J. The Architecture of All Abundance: Seven Foundations to Prosperity. New World Library 2003.

$350 VALUE

GIFT
VOUCHER

FOR ONE PRIVATE HYPNOTHERAPY SESSION
WITH BASS TADROS IN PERSON OR ONLINE

www.basstadros.com | www.forlifecoaching.com.au

REDEEM VOUCHER
T (08) 6113 2078
M +61401273466
E forlife@email.com

www.ingramcontent.com/pod-product-compliance
Lightning Source LLC
Chambersburg PA
CBHW070550300426
44113CB00011B/1849